DISCIPLINE REQUIRED

EDMUND L. DUHAIME

Shooting Star Editions
American Literary Press, Inc.

Discipline Required

Copyright ©2004 Edmund L. Duhaime

All rights reserved under International and Pan-American copyright conventions. No part of this book may be reproduced, stored in a retrieval system, or transmitted in any form, electronic, mechanical, or other means, now known or hereafter invented, without written permission of the publisher. Address all inquiries to the publisher.

Library of Congress
Cataloging in Publication Data
ISBN 1-56167-843-0

Published by

Shooting Star Editions
American Literary Press, Inc.
8019 Belair Road, Suite 10
Baltimore, Maryland 21236

Manufactured in the United States of America

THIS BOOK IS DEDICATED TO MY TWO DAUGHTERS

Mary S. Friese

Norma E. Plant

and

MY FIVE GRANDCHILDREN

Gretchen M. Friese
Thatcher K. Friese
Andrew L. Sagas
Diana L. Sagas
James C. Sagas

THE GOLDEN RULE

EMIAHUDISM:

"Do Not Do unto Others That Which Others Do Not Want Done to Themselves"

L. Dnumde
13:11

This book is divided into 3 sections:

Section One: Foreword(s)

An introduction to the problems we face everyday and what attempts have been made throughout history to correct them. This book's objective is to find the way to do what it takes to fix them.

Section Two: Midword(s)

An alphabetized list of words to provide the keys to unlock the causes of human problems, and seek out the solutions. There are 50 titled words, selected at random, each with its true meaning, usage and its affects upon human behavior.

Section Three: Afterword(s)

Conclusions reached in general but realistic terms, tying all three sections together to form the required goals to achieve civilized behavior.

CONTENTS

SECTION NUMBER ONE
    FOREWORD 1
SECTION NUMBER TWO
    MIDWORD 7
        ANGER 7
        ADMIT 7
        BOASTING 8
        BORROW 8
        CRAVE 8
        CRIME 9
        DISCIPLINE 9
        DEPORTMENT 9
        ENVY 10
        EMPATHY 10
        FRIENDSHIP 11
        FAILURE 11
        GREED 12
        GRATITUDE 12
        HATE 12
        HEALTH 13
        INTEGRITY 13

INSTINCTS	14
JUDGEMENT	15
JOKE	15
KNOWLEDGE	16
KINDNESS	16
LIFE	17
LOVE	17
MUSIC	18
NO	18
NICE	19
OBEY	19
ORDER	20
POLITE	20
POLICE	21
QUIT	21
QUALIFY	22
REQUIREMENT	22
REGULATE	22
STRESS	23
SELFISHNESS	24
TEMPER	24
TRUTH	25
UMPIRE	25
UNCIVIL	26
VICIOUSNESS	26
VIRTUOUS	27

WILD	27
WILL POWER	28
XMAS	28
YES	29
YOU	29
ZEAL	30
ZANY	30

SECTION NUMBER THREE

AFTERWORD	33
THE ESSAY	35
DISCIPLINE	35
CHILDREN'S PAGE	37
ADULT PAGE	39

PREFACE

Let us go to the circus to see the clowns and all of the performers. The trained animals are always a lot of fun to watch, displaying the result of many years of intensive training.

Suppose by some mistake, someone switched one of the lions, and one of the untrained lions, is in the animal act, it would be terrible to watch one of the trained dogs being attacked by that wild, untrained lion unexpectedly. A ruined performance by an undisciplined wild beast.

Keeping that hypothetical example in mind, now let us look at wild humans lacking discipline, that would, not would, but is chaotic also. It happens all the time, every hour, every day, somewhere in the world. If you need any proof, just visit jails, prisons, and death rows in penitentiaries. About all of those inmates did not grow up disciplined.

There are millions more of us who have not received the required, the required discipline either. (Those two words 'required' are written twice intentionally) so, more problems will develop in the future. However, it is possible to avoid those problems by parents insisting upon making their children obey orders of discipline, starting at a very young age, and keeping it up all the time. It is a lot easier to obey parents, than having to be forced to obey society's rules and laws. Just read this book now for guidance. All of it.

SECTION NUMBER ONE
FOREWORD

There are two conditions to be resolved in life. They have been given many identities over the many centuries. I will use the ones most easily recognized. They are, civilized and uncivilized behavior.

Uncivilized living is based upon the make up of the genetic system we are all born with. That included instincts and traits without discipline training; feral behavior.

On the other hand, civilized living is based upon renouncing those feral traits, in favor of having peace and happiness, within a mix of humanity. This we all have to work on in order to achieve it.

Now, in order to achieve this reconstruction, we need to have and use the right tools. They are training (disciplining) and the help of this book, written for that very purpose. Discipline is the bridge over which we must travel from the uncivilized state to the civilized state. Most of us are still in transition on that trip.

There is an old adage which reads, "to be all things to all people." It is intended to be an expression of something which is not possible to do.

However, there is a single word which is, in fact, "all things to all people." That word is discipline. It affects all of us, all the time, but is possible to attain, and must be learned.

A long long time ago that word did not exist, however, the seeds of discipline did exist, in the form of instincts and traits, which live in the genetic system. They still do to this very day.

This is true in countless species, including we humans as well. An example of ancient discipline has been observed by animal parents nudging their cubs physically to push them out of harm's way. Modern humans still do the same thing too, plus using reinforcing words, accompanied by cautious voice tones, an unmistakable exercise of discipline, what else?

The word *discipline* has two main functions, one as a noun, meaning *behavior, strictness, orderliness, conformity, deportment, conduct, courtesy, demeanor,* etc. The other meaning is as a verb, such as *teach, obey, instruct, rule, control, guide, train, punish,* etc.

These few words will set the tone for a full understanding of the importance of the word *discipline*, and how it applies to our every day living. This includes all of us.

A few examples of discipline are listed below:

To obey parents

To respect everybody

To keep promises

To pay bills on time

To keep appointments on time

To always keep one's word

To always be truthful

To respect other people's rights

To obey all laws

To drive courteously

To obey teachers, police, fireman

To practice self control

To be honest and trustworthy

Living a life is considered to be a real challenge, like no other. When buying a new car, a manual comes with it, providing instructions to guide its life. When a child is born, no manual comes with it. The guidance is (or should be) supplied by parents, if you are lucky enough to have parents fully informed, and have the ability to teach what the child must know to live successfully. There are fewer parents, capable in guidance principles, than those parents who lack the ability. Virtually all parents love their children and want what is best for them. However, too many lack the knowledge necessary to achieve their responsibilities.

As a help to provide the knowledge needed to succeed in bringing up children, this book is being written to supply enlightenment about the importance of learning self-control.

This is not only for children but all of us to practice it daily. Never forget our heritage of how our ancestors lived in the uncivilized state, behavior which affects us having to override instincts we inherited. Uncivilized behavior does not mix with civility, and we all need to learn the key to success is through discipline.

The word *discipline* is often interpreted by too many of us as limited to punishment. Sure, punishment is included, but that is only a very small but sometimes a necessary part of the training cycle. Any punishment is mostly temporary and is often not even necessary. Therefore the word *discipline*, if including punishment, would apply on a percentage scale of 100%, would be 1%. The whole of discipline is 99%, other than punishment. Discipline is involved in countless situations, and the following A to Z section spells out many cases of how important it is to know what causes problems in our society.

The A to Z follows:

SECTION NUMBER TWO
MIDWORD

Anger

Meaning: A strong negative emotion.

Usage: It can, and often does aim at some person or a thing. Too often it results in an adverse response, often dangerous. Discipline is lacking here for emotional self-control.

Admit

Meaning: A confession when needed.

Usage: This requires discipline to own up to the truth.

BOASTING

Meaning: An outward expression of one's ego.

Usage: This to be avoided by using discipline (self-control) no one wants to hear it repeatedly.

BORROW

Meaning: Taking from somebody with a promise to return.

Usage: This is to be avoided, but promise kept in the shortest time possible. Requires discipline to prevent any borrowing at all.

CRAVE

Meaning: To want badly.

Usage: Sometimes to the extent of stealing. Stick to the discipline of self-control. Earn the money, then buy.

CRIME

Meaning: Doing something illegal which has laws against it. A direct act of following the wild instincts we are born with, uncivilized behavior. This act is an example of the absence of why discipline is so important to prevent criminal behavior.

DISCIPLINE

Meaning: Good behavior and self-control.

Usage: Absolutely the right way to go, for a happy and peaceful living. Discipline is to life as what a steering wheel is to a car. Necessary!

DEPORTMENT

Meaning: A strong relative of discipline.

Usage: Like a diary of behavior added up over time from which to evaluate living habits. We are judged by our deportment. Obey discipline.

Envy

Meaning: A feeling of discontent and ill will.

Usage: This happens because of another's possessions or advantages. The key here is to learn how to be happy with one's own possessions by the use of self-control, born from discipline.

Empathy

Meaning: The projection of ones own personality into the personality of another person (or thing).

Usage: The meaning of empathy has no trouble bumping into its usage. In a word, like a tool, to arrive at a better understanding of another persons view of a situation. This is commonly known as seeing eye to eye for clear agreement, or even disagreement. A good habit to develop, using discipline as a help.

Friendship

Meaning: A close trustworthy relationship.

Usage: Having a real friendship is an asset to be treasured and protected. This is accomplished by the self-control of avoiding 'using' it as a means to keep getting something for nothing. The best way to preserve a real friendship is to always have self-control of balancing the getting with an equal measure of giving, even to the extent of any giving being more than the getting, but only a little, to avoid any imbalance. It takes self-discipline.

Failure

Meaning: Simply an opposite of success.

Usage: When failure arrives, go back and try again, and again, and again. This takes discipline to achieve, plus patience too. Patience is a part of discipline, and both will bring success.

Greed

Meaning: Never satisfied, and pushing the envelope.

Usage: Taking care of food, shelter, clothing, and health are necessities. When these are satisfied, and a modest surplus is also acquired, more tends to be considered as greed.

Gratitude

Meaning: A feeling of appreciation politely shown.

Usage: Discipline dictates nothing less than just a simple 'thank you'; or sometimes a reciprocal favor. These are an enhancement of a pleasant rapport.

Hate

Meaning: A strong dislike or ill will. To despise.

Usage: Discipline teaches to replace hate with a clear reason to reject hate and replace it with understanding, as hate is self-destructive, and unhealthy.

Health

Meaning: To maintain chemical and physical balance of the body.

Usage: Our bodies do a very good job of running on automatic pilot. However, what we subject our bodies to withstand, will determine the extent of health abuse. Discipline is the control of preventing damage to it, by using moderation in all activities, both mental and physical. Keep away from extremes.

Integrity

Meaning: Behavior to the highest standards.

Usage: To have as a policy, rejecting all forms of misrepresentations of facts, and always truthful, being straightforward, reliable and dependable, always being believable. This condition is born out of discipline.

INSTINCTS

Meaning: What we are born with for survival.

Usage: It is instinctive to blink our eyes automatically, as our eyes need that action, to act like a windshield wiper on a car, it is instinctive to feel hunger pains too. So it is with threats from predators against which our bodies automatically produce sudden shots of adrenaline for immediate extra body strength, for either flight or fight. It is instinctive for a baby learning to crawl or walk. These are only a few of the many instincts we are all born with. We must all be disciplined to learn how to assimilate instincts with civilized living. Sometimes they clash, but learned behavior is our guide.

JUDGEMENT

Meaning: to weigh the facts of any situation to arrive at a conclusion.

Usage: Too many of us jump to conclusions, without having all the facts. Patience, born out of discipline, provides the time required for getting those facts before coming to a decision.

JOKE

Meaning: Something funny to produce laughter.

Usage: We all need a break once in a while from daily doses of stress and tensions. Jokes often provide needed release.

Knowledge

Meaning: A range of information, covering understanding and facts.

Usage: A trained mind can assimilate and add new facts easily. We all acquire knowledge mainly to be able to use it for earning a living. Also for satisfying our curiosity. As we acquire it, we depend upon discipline to monitor it as it enters the brain, to find its correct niche.

Kindness

Meaning: An act of helpfulness to others.

Usage: It is sometimes interpreted as a sign of weakness, and is often taken advantage of. We must discipline our minds to be aware of this possibility, but not to blind us to real appreciated need when it occurs.

LIFE

Meaning: The span of time that our bodies will survive.

Usage: Living a life will depend upon how we choose to live it. It would take a lifetime to describe a whole life here. Simply, however, learn all about the various approaches to it, including this book for guidance. The word is discipline.

LOVE

Meaning: An emotion that describes feelings for others or self.

Usage: It takes a disciplined mind to decide which option to consider while thinking about it. This famous and broad-meaning word, regarding natural physical activity, or in the choice of social mating, following the commitment. These two options are both intertwined, needing an understanding of how self-control must be learned from discipline.

Music

Meaning: Desirable sounds to uplift or for calming.

Usage: There are a great many kinds of music. Almost as many kinds of music, as there are people. It takes discipline to learn and play music. This is a real practice in self-control. Try it, you may like it, but be prepared to have patience for all that practicing.

No

Meaning: Not at all. Opposite of yes.

Usage: This is the very first disciplinary word to be taught to a child; very beginning of discipline. When should it be used initially? At the time a baby starts to crawl, to explore its new world. Using 'no' along with a tone of voice that the child may very well feel fearful of, makes for a double impression on the child's memory. Do not use any other words at the beginning, until the child understands what 'no' means from repeated hearings of it. Then start the vocabulary, one word at a time, until it too sinks in.

Nice

Meaning: Having high standards of conduct.

Usage: To be tactful and considerate of others in dealing with others, to be well mannered and well disciplined. There is only one chance to make a first impression. Make it nice, but be sincere about it like honest.

Obey

Meaning: To follow orders, like laws and instructions.

Usage: The first ones to obey are the parents. They are the ones responsible to teach children early in life, about the importance of obedience. Obedience comes from early discipline.

Order

Meaning: The act of telling someone what to do.

Usage: The order must come from someone who has the authority to do so. It can come from a parent or a teacher, or from other authoritative figures as police, or from laws. In order to know how to respond, requires earlier discipline.

Polite

Meaning: Showing good manners and being considerate.

Usage: Always be thoughtful and well civilized. This behavior is contained in my book titled "Fantastic Blueprint for Living", as the modern golden rule as follows: "Do not do unto others, that which others do not want done to themselves." Read it over and over again and make it a habit to live by it. Then, politeness comes without thinking about it. A real discipline.

Police

Meaning: Guardians of the peace by law and order.

Usage: If it ever happens that all people are civilized and fully disciplined, then we would not need a police department any more. Since we continually need that protection, is proof enough that discipline is sadly lacking, and needs to be practiced daily by all of us.

Quit

Meaning: To stop, give up, and resign, to end.

Usage: In the context of this book, to quit is to quit bad habits. Bad habits must be replaced by good habits. Based upon the rules of discipline. Bad habits are negatives, good habits are positives. Again we all must continue working on discipline which is the key for our best shot at peace and happiness.

Qualify

Meaning: To have what it takes to meet a requirement.

Usage: In order to qualify for anything, we must have obtained a minimum of K-12 schooling, plus experience in any specific field of work one is seeking. Also needed is discipline to satisfy other requirements that a potential job requires, like attitude for instance.

Requirement

Meaning: Something that is necessary to have.

Usage: Within the context of this book, it can only be discipline personified.

Regulate

Meaning: To bring something into conformity.

Usage: Discipline comes to mind as something that is in need to being regulated to the standards established as the means of overriding uncivilized behavior.

Stress

Meaning: Mental and/or physical tension.

Usage: Normal stress, if it exists, is manageable with no adverse effects like shopping, eating, doing dishes, etc. However, excessive stress is the one to avoid, such as a deep frustration, too many debts, constant worry, lack of sleep, too much hate, etc. Controls must be applied in making choices that establish habits of moderation in all of them. This adds up to a desirable discipline. That is what it takes.

Selfishness

Meaning: Comes in three levels.

1. Any act that takes from persons to the detriment of them, like stealing, cheating, killing etc.

2. Any act that takes from persons without being a detriment, like a gift, a favor, or information.

3. Any act that gives something to persons without expecting anything back, like a donation, etc.

In all 3 cases, there is a self-satisfaction, but in a civilized society, avoid number one.

It takes training to become disciplined so as to form the habit, the right choices, all in moderation.

Temper

Meaning: An action of raw behavior completely lacking in self-control.

Usage: Although used as a gimmick to intimidate, it most often results in the opposite often times a fight. All this to be avoided, and replaced with a count to ten, or think twice before the tantrum. Use self-control a habit learned from discipline.

TRUTH

Meaning: True and factual. The real world.

Usage: At times situations become like a bowl of spaghetti, a mixture of bent truths, lies, fiction, misleading, etc. To solve this mess often requires a court and a judge. That is where the truth must be revealed to settle it. We do not inherit truth. It must be taught and learned, as to what it is and practiced, until it becomes a habit. That habit then becomes an integral part of discipline. The truth will make you free.

UMPIRE

Meaning: One who settles controversy and also guides.

Usage: This word is mostly associated with sports activities. But is a synonym of a judge. The umpire also acts as a disciplinarian, and in reality, he is one.

Uncivil

Meaning: To behave in a manner not acceptable in a civilized society.

Usage: A person who acts uncivil is a good example of a person who did not receive (or accept) becoming disciplined when he should have. Maybe never taught either.

Viciousness

Meaning: An inherent instinct used for survival.

Usage: Behavior not acceptable in a civilized society. This ancient instinct was necessary to dissuade predators in time of confrontations. In our civilized society there are still too many throw backs that were never trained (tamed) to override those feral instincts. Just another example of the absolute need for discipline.

Virtuous

Meaning: Morality, thinking goodness, integrity, always polite, considerate, neat, a clean mouth when speaking, etc.

Usage: A virtuous person is always regarded highly and also highly respected. This type of person worked hard at overriding the animal instincts we are all born with.

Thanks to his discipline early in life, which made it all possible. You see, anyone can achieve it.

Wild

Meaning: Not tamed, not trained, uncivilized.

Usage: A person who grew up with no constraints, just raw, and directly according to his uncivilized instincts; a perfect example of an individual who is without self-control, completely lacking discipline.

Will Power

Meaning: Self-control to maintain and practice all good training to become civilized, disciplined.

Usage: When a person has acquired discipline, he must use will power to keep it up, and not be distracted to return to uncivilized behavior. Will power is the engine to keep it going.

Xmas

Meaning: A short version of Christmas.

Usage: For some, it is a celebration time to honor the birth of a man named Jesus Christ. He is alleged to be one who taught a better way to live among others, using compassion (civility) as opposed to uncivilized (animal) behavior. To others, a time to bury the hatchet by exchanging gifts. A common disciplined behavior.

Yes

Meaning: The opposite of no.

Usage: Yes, and its opposite no, are like give and take, like for and against, like up and down, like in and out, like permission and rejection. Parents using discipline, must make choices in guiding their children. They, the parents, must set the example of this quandry themselves, so the children can better understand the correct behavior. Think of it as role modeling.

You

Meaning: You are the baby, the child, the adult, the parent, the guide, and the grandparent. Even the great grand parent. At every stage you play a role that must continue to have civil behavior, for those who look up to you. They then, when it is their turn, if you did your job right, will also be looked up to, to continue being civilized. The continuing process is no less than discipline. It never ends.

ZEAL

Meaning: Anxiety, fervor, eagerness, passionate effort.

Usage: When zeal is added to discipline, then civilized behavior will always prevail.

ZANY

Meaning: Silly, buffoonery, clownish

Usage: This is the offset word. A state of being funny in some ludicrous manner.

After being through the A to Z Section, to detail the construction of discipline, which is a serious work, it is now time to relax from the effort used, and know there is a time for recreation to balance out our humanity. One might say it is the other side of the coin. Have fun.

For many of you readers who like pictures, I have included a pictograph on the next page to display an overview of the A to Z section.

It has been said that a picture is worth a thousand words. This illustration provides a different perspective, but the meaning remains the same.

This Metaphoric

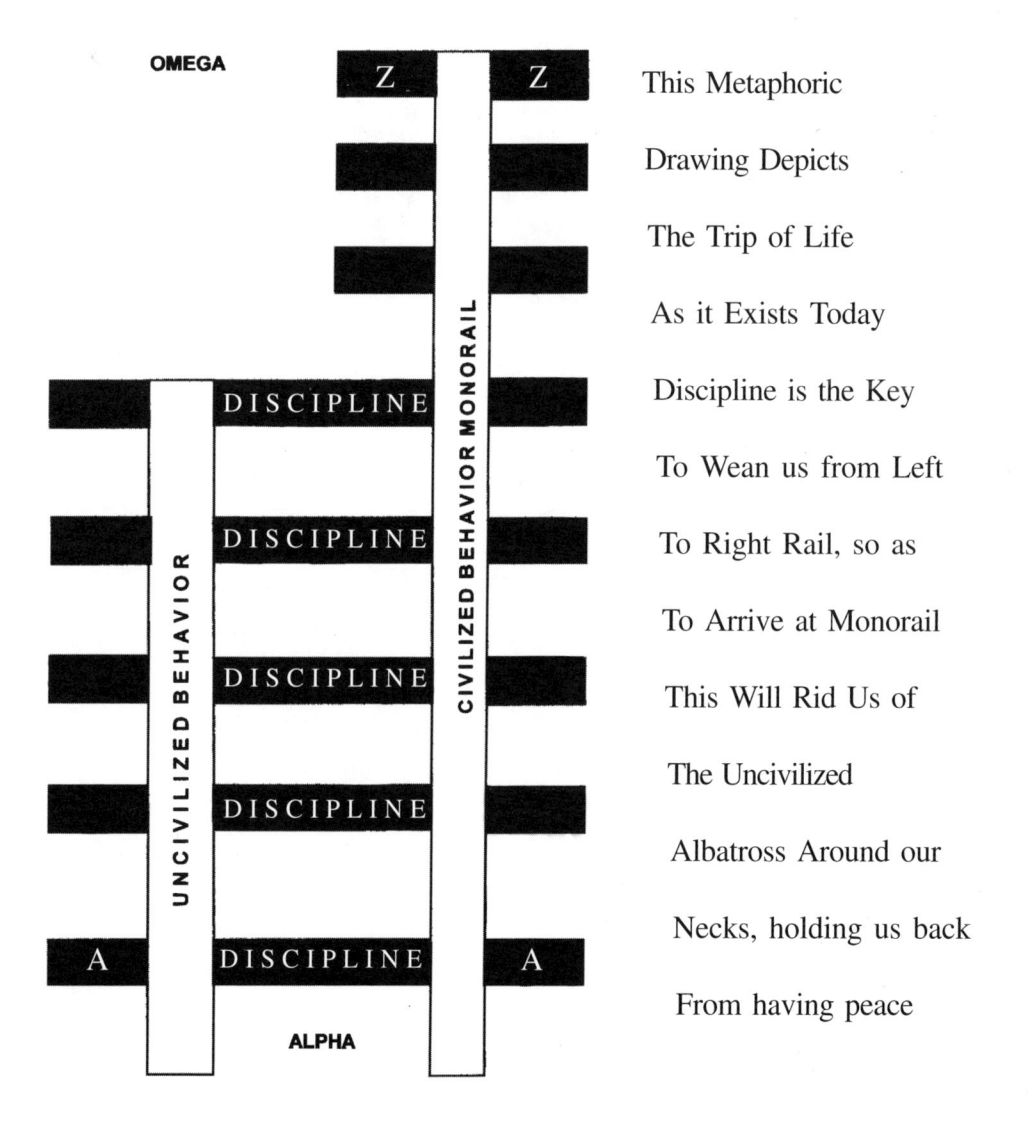

Drawing Depicts

The Trip of Life

As it Exists Today

Discipline is the Key

To Wean us from Left

To Right Rail, so as

To Arrive at Monorail

This Will Rid Us of

The Uncivilized

Albatross Around our

Necks, holding us back

From having peace

SECTION NUMBER THREE
AFTERWORD

Now that you have read this far, you are surely aware of the meaning of the word discipline. Now seems to be a good time to suggest how. When and where would be a good beginning for this necessity which is mostly endless?

A best start is when the baby leans to crawl around to find out, from its instincts, and obviously getting into things. That time has arrived when training must begin. What to do, what to do?? Read on.

Keeping in mind that a baby has only its instincts to go by, it is useless to begin talking a bunch of words. It has no vocabulary, so is time to start a vocabulary using only one word. Repeat, only one word. A brick building begins with only one brick, then only one brick at a time. The baby can take in one word at a time, very often it needs to be repeated until it gets it.

Oh yes, what is that one word? The best choice is the word "No" you will find it convenient to use that one word for years to come. The effectiveness works best when you demand obedience every time you use it. Once that important phase is firmly established, you have saved yourself years of trouble, as obedience to your instructions has been made into a strong habit, as a part of the child's make up. It is a giant step to lay the groundwork in establishing discipline. Also, use a strong tone of voice while using "No" to make an impression on it of something to fear. Its natural instinct of fear will work in your favor. When established firmly, it mostly often prevents the use of spankings, which are best avoided. You see how important that little word "No" is?

In addition to the foregoing, the following essay, which is titled "Discipline" is a true copy taken from my book titled, *Fantastic Blueprint For Living* (Circa 1993) This is an appropriate addendum to this new book titled *Discipline Required*.

THE ESSAY

DISCIPLINE

Quip: What you often wish you didn't have to learn.

Meaning: Training that develops self-control, character, orderliness, and efficiency. Usage: Discipline is a key word in a person's development, from infancy throughout adulthood. It should be understood for what it is, and how it is needed to learn the control of the savagery in most of us. Parents need to insist upon it, and children must learn to obey the parents first of all, as well as to practice the self-control required in a society of people we encounter in life's quest. Also to know how to teach it to their own children, as their turn comes around.

Result: A disciplined person fits well into a civilized society. Discipline is what produced a civilized society in the first place.

Disciplined persons obey laws, learn rules easily, respect other people's rights, etc. What discipline our parents neglected to teach us, we must all learn on our own. It is called self-discipline, and must be practiced daily. How we conduct ourselves toward others is largely determined by how well we are disciplined. We are judged by our actions, and our actions stem from how well we remembered to control emotions in any given circumstances. This comes from our earlier training in many disciplines. Many of us act first, and then think second. We should think first and be disciplined to do so, acting second.

CHILDREN'S PAGE

How do you do! My name is Edmund, and I am glad to meet you all. The subject of discipline in this book is very much a strong part of your lives. You already know this of course. You also know that you have an important responsibility of your part of the work you have to do. When your parents tell you things, it is because they love you, more than any other person alive. Here is your job. When your parents speak, you hear it and you listen to hear what it is all about and your main job is to "receive" it. Meaning, obey their instructions. When you do, they don't have to bug you any more. Good Luck!

ADULT PAGE

You are all beyond the previous children's page. This is why you are on this page. If you find that you are having too many problems with other people, then you must have lost out on something during your childhood. It is never too late to review your progress thus far in your life, to check out the causes, from which solutions can be determined.

This book is written as a help to make as many folks peaceful and happy as possible. A giant step forward comes from knowledge, and I hope the knowledge you have been reading in this book will do it for you. Good Luck.

In conclusion, everyone of us has the onus on our backs to shoulder the responsibility of doing our individual parts to practice self control, and pass on to our children the discipline to achieve peaceful relationships among others. Without discipline there is only anarchy, as lawlessness and disorder in any sphere of activity. In the future, in order to arrive at Utopia, we all have to be disciplined. All of us to renounce uncivilized behavior completely.

My sincere thanks to all of you who took the time to read this book. Special thanks to you parents who stand the best chance to benefit form it. Children need guidance and parents are the first they are exposed to for laying the groundwork for their behavior. Parents are the role models for children to emulate. The hard work it takes to become role models is forgotten while the happy children are happy long after that hard work is forgotten.